DANDELION DREAMS

TALE OF A LITTLE GIRL FROM LANCASTER

PANSETA SMITH

Dedicated with love to Annalise and Bobby and to my mother Auntie Betsy, Salethy, and Auntie Sylvie who raised me. To all who have touched my life, this is for you.

BOOK COVER SUMMARY

"Dandelion Dreams" is a testament to the human spirit's ability to endure, adapt, and flourish, much like the resilient dandelion that dances with the wind. Through its pages, readers will find inspiration, solace, and a reminder that even in the face of adversity, one can bloom beautifully.

It echoes the resilience of the dandelion, scattering seeds of hope and growth for the future.

A celebration of the human capacity to thrive, bloom, and spread beauty, even amidst life's harshest challenges. Allow the wind of these pages to carry you into a world where strength, hope, and the courage to face the unknown become the fertile ground for the blossoming of dreams.

CONTENTS

PROLOGUE

Dandelion Dreams portrays my humble beginning and chronicles my life to the best of my recollection from infancy to maturity. It described the life of a little girl growing up in Lancaster District, Manchester, Jamaica, and what it was like to be raised as a country girl. Dandelion Dreams tells the story of a grandmother's love, sacrifices, determination, and strength of character. This is a nonfiction story, and all the characters are real people, the lives they lived and the challenges they faced are recorded truthfully in this memoir. Throughout my journey, I embraced the valuable lesson that facing challenges is inevitable, but succumbing to defeat is never an option. The memoir underscores the significance of resilience and the transformative power of rising after a setback. This realization has given me the strength to embrace the belief that in this world, I have the capacity to transform into anything and everything that I desire. I've come to understand that I don't need anyone's approval to embark on the journey toward happiness and become the person I aspire to be.

In this heartwarming narrative, follow the compelling journey of a young girl from Lancaster, who faced the daily challenge of walking barefoot to school. The story unfolds against the backdrop of a grandmother's sacrificial love and her courageous battle with cancer, weaving a tapestry of resilience through life's hardships. As the little girl navigates her way from the rural landscapes of Lancaster to the bustling city of Kingston and eventually to the United States, the narrative beautifully illustrates her determination and strength. Through adversity, loss, and change, the story captures the essence of resilience, highlighting the triumph of the human spirit. This poignant tale is a testament to the enduring power of love, sacrifice, and the indomitable will to forge one's path against all odds."

CHAPTER ONE

ROOTS IN LANCASTER

The District of Lancaster sits on Carpenter's Mountain in Manchester. There, in a tiny house with an outside kitchen made with wattle and daub on the hill, my character was formed.

Wattle and Daub were used to make walls and buildings, in which a plaited frame of wooden strips called wattle is daubed with a sticky material usually made of wet soil, clay, sand animal waste, and straw. That small house on the hill has carved lives and shaped many characters. I lived in that house with Salethy, my brother Danny and Cousin Tony throughout my childhood. My mother was living in Kingston, the capital of Jamaica at that time. Salethy's mother, whom we called Muma, also lived on the same property, in her own house closer to the main entrance.

It's a beautiful tradition to assign names as a mark of respect, especially within the cultural context of acknowledging and honoring elders. In the case of "SaRose" and "Salethy," the prefix "Sa" functions as a title equivalent to "Sister." This practice reflects a deep-seated cultural respect for elders, emphasizing the importance of acknowledging and showing deference to siblings and individuals within the community.

Muma, my great-grandmother, originally hailed from Mandeville, the capital of Manchester, and bore the name Rose Bird. However, within the district, she was affectionately known as SaRose. Born to Charlie Bird and an unnamed mother who shared the Bird surname, Muma's familial roots were grounded in Mandeville.

In her youth, Muma entered matrimony with Pupa, Joseph Pinnock, a union that led her to Lancaster. This marriage bore fruit to four daughters: Leathy Ann affectionately known as Saleathy, Elfreda, Bernice, and Minna

Elfreda, Muma's second daughter, got married to Claudius Beaumont, who everyone fondly called Buckom. Their union produced a family comprising sons Charles, David, Adrian, Edgar, Herbert, and Philmore, along with daughters Rose, Esther, and May.

In contrast, Bernice, another of Muma's daughters, had a smaller but cherished family, with two children named Norma and Samuel. Norma, in turn, expanded the lineage with Donna and Dave, who stand as my second cousins.

Dandelion Dreams: *Tale of a Little Girl from Lancaster*

Mina, the fourth daughter, 'wash belly', remained unmarried and did not bear any children, contributing her unique narrative to the family tapestry.

Every family member's story, whether through marriages and children or personal paths, adds unique shades to the collective history of Muma's.

Although, I never had the opportunity to meet Pupa, family narratives paint a vivid picture of a robust Black man who sought employment in Cuba, a common venture during those times, when boat travel was the primary means, given the limited prevalence of air travel. The day of his funeral carried unique rituals, etching lasting memories for his descendants. Each child and grandchild received a white handkerchief containing a lock of Pupa's hair. A solemn ceremony unfolded as they were instructed to open the caskets, call out their names, declaring, "Pupa, I am done with you," and placed the handkerchief in his hand. The intensity of fear associated with these tasks was so profound that Salethy had to perform them on behalf of the family. This ceremonial practice aimed at formalizing a symbolic separation, ensuring that Pupa's spirit would not return to haunt their lives.

Muma earned a living by breaking rocks; during that era, there was no technology for producing gravel used in construction, so people had to manually break large stones into the necessary gravel for road paving. The Public Works department in Newport supplied the stones, delivered in a large yellow truck that would drop a load at the gate.

Muma would efficiently break up the stones, and each week, she would receive another load for processing. The same truck would then transport the broken gravel. The details of her payment method were unknown to me.

As a child, I observed Muma sitting on a heap of stones with a small hammer in the mornings, before I left for school. When I returned, she would still be in the same spot, diligently breaking away at the stones. I also noticed white spots on the side of her neck and her fingers. At the time, I didn't understand, but later in life, I learned that she had vitiligo. Interestingly, her only brother, Louis, also had the same condition.

Muma was well-educated and possessed a strong command of the English language. She had been taught Latin in school and could write in Old English. During my childhood, she even taught me how to write Old English in the dirt with a simple stick. Muma tended to keep to herself.

Dandelion Dreams: *Tale of a Little Girl from Lancaster*

Apart from occasional visits from her daughters, I seldom witnessed any friends coming to see her. After Pupa died, she lived alone. By the time I moved away from Lancaster to live with my mother, Muma was still living alone.

She had a habit of retiring to bed every night as the sun set. Despite her solitude, Muma remained sharp and could distinguish us by name based on our footsteps as we passed by her apartment on our way to Salethy's. She would call us by name when we passed by her tiny apartment. She continued to live independently in her own apartment within the same yard until she passed away at the age of 102. When I was living with my mother at 15 Texton Rd., in Kingston, we received a telegram informing us of her death.

Although I didn't attend her funeral, I felt a sense of sadness knowing that she was gone, and I wouldn't see her again.

CHAPTER TWO
SALETHY'S EMBRACE: A GRANDMOTHER'S SACRIFICE, LOVE, AND MENTORSHIP

Salethy, a woman of exceptional beauty and a kind, humble nature, played a crucial role in shaping who I am. Her kindness and gentleness have had a lasting impact on me, and I credit much of my positive qualities to the love and guidance she provided.

Even without the opportunity for formal education, Salethy possessed a wealth of knowledge gained through her life experiences. As the eldest of four girls, she took on the responsibility of caring for her siblings. Despite never marrying, Salethy embraced motherhood and raised seven children. James, Kado, and Birdie were born from her union with Rudolph Daley from the same parish. After his passing, Salethy found love again with George Clarke from Lancaster, and together they had Mirian also called Sylvie, Betsy, and Janie.

Dandelion Dreams: *Tale of a Little Girl from Lancaster*

Sylvie has two children; Beverly and Orville, whom we called T. Betsy my mother had three children, Danny, my sister Sheryl, and myself, whom they called Sissy. Janie also had two children Tony and Glenn.

During this time, George Clarke had affairs with other women in the district, leading to the birth of Linda and Nathan. Additionally, Salethy had a child with another man known as Mass Will.

Mass Will, Salethy's lover, was known for walking barefoot with a crocus bag on his shoulder. Occasionally, Mass Will sought our help in harvesting produce on his farm in Enfield, a neighboring district. We willingly took on this task. Located around three and a half miles from Lancaster, the farm was a vital source of food for Salethy. During holidays, Mass Will would also provide meat, which, given the absence of a refrigerator, Salethy preserved by rubbing it with salt and hanging it over a wood fire to ensure its preservation.

Salethy gracefully assumed the role of nurturing, her grandchildren Danny, Tony, and myself, imparting unconditional love and valuable mentorship.

She was very skilled and talented so she would make our mugs from condensed milk tins also. So, when our enamel mugs chipped and began to leak, she would substitute it with the tin mugs.

We had to fetch our own water from the parish tank because we didn't have running water. Fortunately for us, a water hydrant and community pipe were installed right outside our gate.

Since we lacked a tank, we had to make multiple journeys with our containers to fill our two concrete drums. To keep our water clean, we covered it with a shiny piece of metal. But when it rained, we happily took off the cover, letting the water soak up the rain. This easy trick saved us from going to the pipe to get water and added a touch of nature's colors to our everyday tasks.

There was also a little pond at the back of our house. Danny and Tony used to swim in the pond and take baths when it rained and catch clean rainwater. I also recall a particular day, when Lancaster District experienced heavy rainfall, accompanied by hail descending from the skies. Salethy, demonstrating her resourcefulness, encouraged us to collect some of the hail to serve as ice for cooling our beverages. This incident serves as a testament to her adeptness in making the most of every available opportunity.

CHAPTER THREE
HARVESTING GOLD: A CHAPTER OF MORNING COFFEE AND CHERRY PULP DELIGHTS

There was a coffee walk at the side of our house; during harvest time we would pick the ripe red coffee pulp and put it in a mortar and use the pestle to grind the pulps.

Then we would put the beans to dry on a sheet of zinc in the backyard. After drying the beans Salethy would parch them on wood fire. We would then grind the beans again in the mortar using the pestle. Salethy would then boil a pot of coffee on the fire and strain it through a piece of cloth. Every morning, we would get a mug of coffee before school. When we were reaping the coffee as kids, Danny, Tony, and I would eat the cherry pulp.

There was also a cho cho (chayote) bed on our property. Our dinner was mostly cho cho with salt fish, curry cho cho or anything with cho cho. Salethy always made a delicious meal with the cho cho she grew on the property.

Dandelion Dreams: *Tale of a Little Girl from Lancaster*

When it was the pimento season, we went into the bushes from early mornings after our cup of coffee to pick pimento.

We stored the pimento in a big metal container that once held cooking oil. When we were out harvesting and hungry before having enough for the day, we would also snack on the pimento berries. Salethy would sell them tFo merchants, providing us with our source of income.

The land we lived on was incredibly fruitful, offering oranges, tangerines, grapefruit, and star apples. We'd climb the trees and enjoy these fruits to our hearts' content. At times, we indulged so much that when we jumped down, you could hear the fruit juice bubbling in our stomachs.

We also had a jackfruit tree at the side of our house. When the jackfruit was ripe it would drop from the tree. We would be so excited and eat the fruit then roast the seed in the fire. My favorite fruit was the grapefruit. I would cut it in half and take out the inside, placed it in a mug and eat it with condensed milk. When we did not have condensed milk, I would use sugar to make my favorite drink. Salethy once told me the reason I loved grapefruit was because when I was a baby, they took me to the tree and chopped on the tree just above my head. As the tree flourished, I would grow and become healthy like the tree. It is also customary for them to plant the umbilical cord (navel string) at the root of a tree and that is to make the baby grow and flourish like the tree. My navel string was planted at the root of a grapefruit tree.

The parcel of land next to our house was very green and pretty with a soft type of grass that is known as Pangola or (Digitaria eriantha). This is a tropical grass and is used extensively for grazing. So, farmers would tie their goats and cows for grazing on the Pangola grass. We on the other hand would pull the grass with our bare hands and put it to dry.

Salethy, with her resourcefulness, would skillfully sew together flour bags, creating large sacks that served as makeshift mattresses for our beds. These mattresses, stuffed with soft grass, provided us with a surprisingly comfortable nights' sleep. It felt like having a brand-new mattress whenever we made one, a process we repeated as needed, depending on grass availability.

Inside our humble abode were two wooden beds and a table, adorned with a charming "home sweet home" lamp that Salethy carefully maintained.

Dandelion Dreams: *Tale of a Little Girl from Lancaster*

This lamp illuminated our nights with a warm glow. In addition to this, Salethy ingeniously crafted another lamp from a condensed milk tin, complete with a wick from Mr. Meikle's shop. This outdoor and kitchen-friendly lamp served various purposes.

My daily chores included sweeping the house floor with bush brooms and tending to the chimmy, the container used for overnight urination. If we had to throw water or anything outside during the night we had to call out to the ancestors, "wata a top, wata a bottom, look out" This serves as a form of communication with the spirits, specifically alerting the ghosts of the intention of disposing of water outside the door.

Adjacent to the kitchen, there was another room primarily functioning as a pantry, storing our food supplies. For our convenience, an outdoor pit latrine served our daytime needs, while the tin lamp aided nighttime excursions when necessary.

This insight into our daily living arrangements highlights Salethy's knack for making the best out of what we had, creating a warm and functional home environment.

Tony and Danny had the task of venturing into the bushes to gather firewood, a crucial resource for Salethy to light our cooking fire with kerosene oil. To ignite the fire, we would blow on the firewood until it blazed. Nightly, we had the responsibility of clearing the ashes from the fire site to ensure a successful ignition in the morning.

Every Saturday, Salethy would send us to the shop to purchase one quart of kerosene oil, essential for both the lamps and the firewood. Despite our humble circumstances, we possessed a small transistor radio that allowed us to tune in to Radio Jamaica, Radio Fusion (RJR), and the Jamaica Broadcasting Corporation (JBC). These broadcasts provided a source of entertainment and connection to the outside world. Our radio was stuck on RJR. I am not sure if Salethy just loved RJR, or if she was unable to change the station.

We could not miss Dulcimena, which was a story about a young country girl who moved to Kingston in search of opportunities. Dulcimena was aired every night after the prime-time news. I remember that when they were making the death announcements on the radio how I would be afraid and curl up beside Salethy. I do not understand now why I was afraid.

At the end of each school year, Salethy would give us a cleanser 'wash out.' She thought that it was good to give us a fresh start and purge our bodies for the new school year. There was a Dandelion plant at the side of the house. So, worm medicine and dandelion were what we had to consume. Dandelion was supposed to enhance focus and open the mind.

She used the dandelion to make tea and we had to drink it for a whole week to cleanse our bodies. I still remember vividly that summer when I contracted the mumps. It was Salethy, our intelligent and compassionate grandmother, who helped me with her folk cures, I will never forget how she mixed ashes, two cocoa leaves, and a piece of string to create a makeshift cure that she thought would assist with my symptoms. Salethy used a combination of herbs with recognized therapeutic qualities to make a strong tea in addition to the cocoa leaves. She believed that guava leaves, jack in the bush, dandelion root, leaf of life may strengthen my immune system and speed up my healing. To my astonishment, the herbal remedy worked wonders, and my recovery journey progressed far more rapidly than I had anticipated. The need for frequent visits to the doctor became obsolete, all thanks to Salethy's home remedies. Salethy's profound understanding of tapping into the therapeutic potential of nature deeply impacted me. Her ability to harness the healing power of natural remedies not only alleviated my physical ailment but also instilled in me a newfound appreciation for the holistic and age-old wisdom of herbal cures.

Salethy kept imparting her vast knowledge despite the changing of the seasons. I remember another time she made a calming tea out of the King of the Forest leaves mixed with peppermint, fever grass, and leaf of life.

There was a Physic Nut Tree at the side of our house that we would cut on Good Fridays, and it would bleed. Salethy told us that it was the same tree that the cross of Jesus was made from and that was the reason it bled on Good Friday. I cannot remember if we ever cut the tree another day to see if it would bleed. We had so much confidence in Salethy as children so, whatever she said that we were completely satisfied with and took as gospel.

Salethy used a creative method to bake her potato pudding, also called "pone" using fire on top and underneath the pans since she didn't have an oven. This unique technique, called "hell a top, hell a bottom, hallelujah in the middle," highlighted her resourcefulness and determination in overcoming challenges in her culinary endeavors. Salethy had a coup at the back of the house where she raised chickens. They were let out to go to roost at night. Ironically, she did not eat chicken, however, during the holiday season we would enjoy a meal of home-grown chicken. The chickens were fed with corn and sometimes they would let the chickens out of the coup to go into the gardens to find food. The job to kill the chicken for dinner was for Danny and Tony again. One would take the chicken out of the coup, place it under a big basin with the neck of the chicken out. One would put a knee on the basin and the other would chop off the neck with a machete. I would always stay far away when they were killing the fowl because it would flatter for several minutes even with the head cut off. Salethy would then put the fowl in a kerosene tin with boiling water for a few minutes, then we would remove all the feathers. She would prepare a rich and healthy dinner of rice and peas with chicken.

CHAPTER FOUR
"FOOTPRINTS OF FEAR: NAVIGATING CHILDHOOD ADVENTURES AT FRANKFIELD PRIMARY SCHOOL"

My years at Frankfield Primary School were not without adventure. The school was in Frankfield District which was approximately three miles from our house in Lancaster. We had to walk barefooted to and from school every day. Salethy told us to be careful while walking to school and beware of 'Black heart men.' They were supposed to be bad men, who would steal children and cut out their hearts and drink the blood. I do not know if Salethy told us that, so we would not talk to strangers, but we were so afraid and ran into nearby bushes to hide if we heard a vehicle coming. Salethy also encouraged us to walk in groups and never to take the long walk alone. When I was in Grade One at Frankfield School there was a rumor that a coffin was travelling on two legs looking for Mr. Brown, so we should be on the lookout for the coffin and walk in groups. I know how ridiculous that sounds now but at that time we were terrified and would rush home after school in fear of any contact with the coffin. If that was not enough stress on us as children, there was a mad man named "Youtie" who used to run us down in the evenings when we were going home. We were so afraid of Youtie that we would try to outrun him and rush home to safety. On a normal day, when he was not running us home, the boys would use grass straws and catch lizards.

They would run after the girls they like and try to put lizards on them. My big brother Danny and Cousin Bev were there to protect me, so I was not afraid. I vividly remember an incident, when Danny, on one occasion, caught a lizard and placed it on me. To my surprise, I realized that the lizard did not bite me. Danny explained that he did this to demonstrate that lizards are not harmful. Since that day, my fear of lizards has completely dissipated.

Lunchtime at Frankfield Primary School was a delightful experience characterized by the well-prepared cuisine offered at the school canteen. The menu prominently featured expertly crafted meals, with a focus on Bulgur—a dish I relished, especially when prepared without any meat.

During recess, we had a blast playing dandy shandy, and the boys got creative with a makeshift cricket game using oranges and flat boards from the school compound. Amidst the fun, my mind was occupied with the mental ability section to follow under the poinciana tree with Miss Coombs. Miss Combs was very strict and carried a leather strap on her shoulder. Fearful of her spanking, I diligently memorized multiplication tables which were at the back of our exercise books in my head while enjoying the break.

I consistently set aside funds to purchase culinary delights such as Johnny cake, coconut drops, and blue draws from Miss Estelle. Situated on the school compound, Miss Estelle operated a small stall, where she catered to the culinary preferences of the school children by offering delectable desserts. I can still relish the delightful memory FFof the scrumptious Johnny Cake, expertly crafted with baking soda and beautifully shaped by her skillful hands.

My first school trip was to one of the parishes in the rural areas, I do not remember the exact location, but it was to the beach. Salethy, Auntie Sylvie, Bev, Danny, and Tony were also on the trip. My very protective grandmother sat beside me on the bus ride which was approximately two hours 'drive from Lancaster. We sang folk songs as we travelled while being very anxious, sometimes cheering the driver to drive faster. When we finally reached our destination, I could not contain my excitement because it was my first experience at the beach. There are no beaches in Manchester. The only large body of water is the neighboring Alligator Pond, which is a fishing village where fishermen launched their boats to catch fishes.

I was afraid of the water and did not want to go in. After much prompting from my cousin, Bev, and brother Danny I decided to venture into the water. The water was blue and warm. When it was time for lunch, I did not want to come out of the water because I was having so much fun riding the waves. Salethy and Auntie Sylvie did not go into the water, but they served as our personal lifeguards and coaches. If we ever go one toe further than the knee height that we were instructed, we could hear them shouting our names to come back ashore. We assembled for lunch at one of the spots on the sand under a small hut. Salethy and Auntie Sylvie prepared our lunches, which were rice with red peas and chicken that Salethy and Auntie Sylvie prepared from earlier in the morning and packed for the trip. I slept in Salethy's lap the whole ride home exhausted from the long ride and had so much fun on the beach.

I was placed third from a class of thirty-two in both grade One and Two. Rita Evans was 1st and Merline Brown came second. I received Academic Achievement for grades Two and Three and was given prizes at the Annual Prize Giving Ceremonies. My cousin Bev was very bright and always placed first in her class. One of my prizes was a book about Zarius' Daughter. I was so happy and ran home to read the book for Salethy.

Despite her inability to read, Salethy made it her mission to ensure that I could. Her encouragement took the form of asking me to read stories to her and our neighbor, Ms. Amy. Picture this: the rustic wattle and daub kitchen illuminated by the soft glow of the tin lamp, with the three of us nestled together at night. As I read stories aloud, they, in turn, shared their own tales with me.

One narrative from Salethy has etched itself into my memory. It was about a mother and her son. In this emotional tale, the mother refrained from punishing her son for his wrongdoings. However, the consequences unfolded when he found himself in serious trouble, landing him in jail. During a visit, he took a drastic step, biting off his mother's ears, and conveyed a powerful message, "You should have trained me properly, or I wouldn't be here." The story served as a poignant lesson, emphasizing the importance of not spoiling children, and the significance of proper guidance from parents. Salethy's storytelling not only enriched my reading experience but also imparted timeless wisdom that lingers in my heart.

My Grade three teacher was Miss Forbes, and she too had a strap on her shoulders. We were introduced to decimals and had to recite the fraction table which was also at the back of the exercise book. On Friday afternoons, the lower grades would join the upper grades, and we would sing songs in rounds and play games. At those times, we were happy and saw the good side of our principal. But during devotions we would assemble in the large auditorium, and we had to sing the school song. "We build our School on Thee Oh Lord." He would walk around the auditorium and look at every one of the approximately one hundred of us attending at the time. Woe unto the student who did not know the school song or the "Our Father Prayer." After devotion he would give the announcements. At the end of each school year, the Ministry of Education would send representatives to the school to observe the teaching and assess the school. He would tell us ahead of time, so that we could wear clean uniforms, also shoes and socks for the visit. Our uniforms were blue tunics and white blouses for the girls and khaki suits for the boys.

The teachers would also prepare their lesson plans and brief us on what we should know. They would also rearrange the class so that we would not sit beside our friends, which would eliminate talking. The week before, our best work would be on display in the classrooms. We had to be on our best behavior because if the school lost points, then the budget would be cut.

We also had our Annual Sports Day at Frankfield School, and we all had to participate in an event to score points for our houses. My main event was the high jump, they would put a long piece of stick placed at various levels on two posts at each end. We would then run and try to get over the stick without touching it.

I did well in grades 1 - 4, which was all the time I spent at Frankfield Primary School. My Cousin Bev passed the 9th Grade Achievement Test and earned a place at the prestigious Manchester High School.

CHAPTER FIVE

"ROGUE AND RUMOR: EXPLORING THE UNCONVENTIONAL LIFE OF GEORGE"

George, my maternal grandfather, was an intriguing character, though I never had the chance to meet him. Stories circulated about his aggressive nature, earning him a reputation as the district's most notorious con artist. According to reliable sources, George made a living by training and selling dogs. Rumors circulated that he would even sell the same dog to two different individuals. For instance, he might sell a dog to a man in Lancaster and then steal it back to sell to another person in Ellen St, a nearby district.

Known for his fighting spirit and treacherous demeanor, George was not well-liked in the community. George's legacy isn't one of conventional adoration, but rather of gritty resilience and unwavering resolve. In the face of adversity, he stood firm, refusing to be swayed by the opinions of others. His fighting spirit was legendary, a testament to his unwillingness to back down from any challenge, no matter how daunting.

Despite his treacherous demeanor, there's a certain respect that accompanies George's name. He wasn't one to sugarcoat his intentions or mince words, and while his methods may have been unconventional, they were undeniably effective. His actions spoke volumes, leaving an imprint on the fabric of our community that will endure for generations to come.

In the grand tapestry of our history, George's presence looms large, a reminder that strength isn't always measured by popularity, but by the impact one leaves behind. His legacy is etched in the very foundation of our community, a testament to the power of resilience, determination, and the unwavering spirit of a true fighter.

In those days when a disruptive individual passed away, undertakers would secure their big toes to prevent their spirit ("duppy") from wandering. In George's case, all of his toes were tied to ensure his duppy remained still.

Uncle Nathan inherited some of his father's traits and proved to be a nuisance in the district. Exhibiting the same aggressive tendencies, he would rough us up whenever we encountered him on the streets. Unemployed, he often occupied the pavement near Mr. Meikle's shop in the square, seeking alcohol from passersby.

He would threaten to beat Danny and Tony without cause, insisting that they should learn to love and appreciate their big uncle. While he never physically harmed me, I lived in fear of him. The childhood abuses we endured were a consequence of our mothers' absence from our lives.

The abuses that I suffered, sexually and physically, I kept to myself, because I was ashamed and afraid to talk about them. Most times the abusers would drive fear in me which makes it hard to tell on them.

The abuse originated from family members whom we admired and respected, making it difficult to voice any grievances against them. At times, the mistreatment seemed so commonplace that we internalized it as normal and, so, chose to suffer in silence.

CHAPTER SIX

"MOTHER-DAUGHTER
DYNAMICS"

My relationship with my mother, affectionately known as Aunty Betsy during my childhood in Lancaster, is truly unique and special. While our bond may differ from traditional mother-daughter relationships, it is enriched with its own distinctive qualities that make it extraordinary. Aunty Betsy has been a source of unwavering support, understanding, and love throughout my upbringing. Her nurturing presence has played a vital role in shaping the person I am today. Our connection, though unconventional, has provided me with a sense of security and belonging that goes beyond societal norms. I am grateful for the warmth and care she has consistently shown, making our bond a cherished and beautiful part of my life's journey.

My mother attended the Snowden All Age School alongside her siblings. Upon completing her education at the age of 14, she relocated to St Mary under the care of Miss Val's brother to assume the role as 'Nanny" However, her adolescence took an unexpected turn as she became a mother at a young age when she had my brother Danny. In the face of profound adversity, she endured a deeply harrowing experience, subjected to rape by the very individual entrusted with her care and protection. This distressing ordeal unfolded within the context of her selfless dedication to tending to the needs of his children, a responsibility she assumed with unwavering commitment.

The trauma inflicted upon her was not merely physical; it encompassed emotional and psychological dimensions, leaving indelible scars on the fabric of her being. The betrayal by the person who should have served as a protector of security and support, instead, became a source of anguish and despair.

Her return to Lancaster marked the beginning of a journey supported by Salethy's resolute care and understanding, providing a stable foundation for her role as a mother. I came on the heels of my brother three years later when she was still a teenager. I can well imagine the hardship she faced with limited resources as my father at the time had several other children and was not providing any support. Faced with the responsibility of providing for two children on her own, she embarked on a journey to Kingston in search of a better life. When I left Salethy and was living with her in Kingston we had a good relationship until Brady came in the picture. My recollections bring to mind Brady, who, at that time, was in a relationship with Shirley—a fellow resident within the same tenement yard located at 15 Texton Rd. The dynamics of our previously positive association shifted with Brady's presence, marking a turning point in our interactions and the atmosphere within our shared living space.

Prior instances, notably during our time at Texton Rd, resurfaced, revealing a pattern of abusive behavior from Brady. Witnessing his aggression towards Shirley, coupled with instances of verbal abuse and physical altercations, left an indelible impact on my perception of him.

The intensity of my emotions during these moments cannot be understated, marked by a profound dislike towards Brady and a visceral desire to protect my mother from harm. These experiences instilled a sense of rage and helplessness, leading to a fervent wish to eradicate the threat he posed. In sharing these difficult experiences, it is essential to underscore the gravity of the emotional toll endured and the imperative of seeking support and intervention in situations of abuse.

Dandelion Dreams: *Tale of a Little Girl from Lancaster*

While, the chapters of my life include painful experiences, the invaluable lessons gleaned from them have shaped me into a stronger and more confident individual. The void left by Salethy's departure initially made me feel like a lost little girl. However, as the years passed, I came to understand that the relationship with my mother was intricately linked to her own internal struggles and brokenness. The emotional and physical distance experienced during my formative years had a profound impact on the dynamics of our relationship, imposing a considerable toll.

Brady's presence brought additional challenges. His laziness and expectations for financial support created strain between us as mother and daughter.

In contemplating my life journey, I understand that each trial has contributed to my growth, reinforcing the importance of resilience and empathy in navigating life's complexities. In the midst of the shortcomings I pointed out about my mother, it's crucial to recognize the profound care she had for me.

She was very generous a trait that has passed on to us her children. I watched her struggles as a child and was always at awe as her strength and unyielding resilience shine brightly. I've observed her effortlessly dismantling barriers and conquering challenges that seemed insurmountable to others. Her unwavering determination to reach her aspirations is undeniable.

Although my upbringing may not have been affluent in material possessions, I treasure something far more invaluable – the profound love of my grandmother. The indomitable strength of my mother, exemplified through her resilient journey from Lancaster to Kingston and subsequently to the United States, stands as a testament to her remarkable fortitude amidst formidable challenges. I extend my sincere admiration for her unwavering tenacity, which enabled her to navigate through the adversities that punctuated her path.

The sacrifices she made on my behalf transcend quantifiable measures, embodying a depth of devotion that surpasses any conceivable metric. Her dedication to ensuring my well-being and opportunities for a brighter future underscores a selflessness that is both profound and awe-inspiring. It is within the crucible of her sacrifices that I find the truest expression of maternal love, a force that eclipses any other worldly attachment.

Dandelion Dreams: *Tale of a Little Girl from Lancaster*

In contemplating the magnitude of her journey and the depths of her sacrifices, my affection for her transcends mere sentiment; it assumes the form of an enduring bond that resonates with gratitude and profound respect. Her resilience has not only shaped my understanding of perseverance but has also become an enduring source of inspiration, motivating me to overcome challenges with a similar determination.

As I reflect on the arduous path she traversed, I am reminded of the unparalleled strength inherent in maternal love. Her journey, fraught with obstacles, is a living testament to the profound impact that a mother's sacrifices can have on shaping the destiny of her child. In saluting her strength, I not only acknowledge the formidable journey she undertook but also express profound gratitude for the unwavering love and sacrifices that have become the bedrock of my existence.

On the tragic day of my mother's passing, I stood by her bedside, holding onto hope and fervently praying for a miraculous recovery from the severe stroke that had befallen her. Despite my desperate yearning for her to remain with us, it became evident that her journey had reached its conclusion.

Reflecting on her life, I find solace in the fact that she faced life's challenges with resilience and conquered them. Now, my deepest wish is for her to find blissful repose under the comforting wings of Jesus, immersed in eternal peace. As her earthly journey concludes, I confidently affirm, "Mother, you have done well. Sleep on, dear mother, until we reunite." Despite any circumstances, she bestowed upon me the gift of life and imparted invaluable lessons that will forever shape me. She serves as the catalyst behind the success of her three children and gave us the opportunity to move to the United States for a better life.

As I bid farewell to her physical presence, I was confronted with a tumultuous array of emotions. The immediate impact was overwhelming, a storm of grief, sadness, and disbelief that engulfed my entire being. Her death was not just the loss of a beloved family member but a seismic shift that fundamentally altered my sense of self and my place in the world.

One of the most profound changes was to my sense of identity. Our relationship, like many, had its complexities and unresolved issues. There were times when I longed to mend and improve our connection, to fix what was broken or strained between us. Her passing left me grappling with the realization that some things would forever remain unresolved, and this brought about a deep, introspective examination of who I was without her.

Over the years, our relationship had evolved, sometimes growing distant, other times reconnecting with a renewed sense of understanding. Yet, regardless of the ebbs and flows of our interactions, there was always an underlying, steadfast sense of safety and security in having her presence in my life. She was a constant, an anchor that, despite the occasional storm, provided a sense of stability and belonging.

Her death, however, left an irreplaceable void in my heart. It was not just her physical absence but the loss of that intrinsic feeling of safety and the knowledge that there was someone who cared for me unconditionally. This void has been a constant companion, a silent reminder of her absence that pervades my everyday life.

Emotional and Psychological Transformation

In the wake of her passing, I experienced a profound emotional and psychological transformation. The initial grief evolved over time, sometimes manifesting as an acute sense of loneliness and other times as a lingering, background sorrow. This journey through grief has taught me the fluidity of emotions, how they can shift and change unexpectedly, yet persist as an ever-present undercurrent.

Social and Interpersonal Dynamics

The loss also reshaped my social and interpersonal dynamics. Relationships with family members and friends were tested and redefined. Some bonds strengthened as we shared our grief and supported one another, while others became strained under the weight of loss. This period revealed the true nature of many relationships in my life, highlighting those built on genuine connection and support.

Coping and Behavioral Adjustments

In learning to cope with her absence, I have had to develop new mechanisms to manage stress and emotional pain. Engaging in creative outlets and establishing new routines also became vital in filling the void left by her death.

Existential and Spiritual Reflections

Her passing prompted deep existential and spiritual reflections. Confronting mortality so closely led me to ponder life's broader meanings and my purpose within it.

Dandelion Dreams: *Tale of a Little Girl from Lancaster*

This exploration has been both a source of solace and a path to greater self-awareness, helping me find a sense of peace amidst the chaos of loss.

Personal Growth and Resilience

Through this journey of grief, I have discovered an inner resilience I was previously unaware of. The necessity of managing life without my mother has forced me to become more independent and self-reliant. It has also prompted me to reevaluate my priorities and values, leading to a more intentional and meaningful approach to life.

Her memory continues to guide me, serving as a reminder of the love and lessons she imparted. While the void she left will never be filled, it has become a part of my journey, shaping who I am today and who I strive to become. The experience of losing my mother, though profoundly painful, has ultimately been a catalyst for significant personal growth and a deeper appreciation for the fragility and beauty of life.

I am certain that she navigated the journey of life exceptionally. Despite the adversities we faced, I will forever appreciate the profound teachings she shared throughout our time together.

CHAPTER SEVEN
SHARED INSIGHTS AND
STRENGTHENED BONDS

My father, Ronald Morgan, was a highly successful figure in the district of Lancaster. As a scholar, he served as the Superintendent of Public Works in Newport, Manchester. His influence extended widely, earning him the admiration of many, particularly the young ladies in the district. In addition to his professional achievements, he held significant roles as a Justice of the Peace, Politician, and a Minister of Religion. Remarkably, he fathered sixteen children.

While I don't have a precise ranking among the siblings, I recall having an older sister, Beverly, who resided next door to Salethy, and a brother, Ashley, who was born just months apart from me. Ashley's mother lived approximately one-fourth of a mile from our home in Lancaster. Subsequently, Ronald entered into a marriage with Sissy from the same parish, resulting in the birth of Lowell, Kenneth, Cecil, Lorna, and Vanessa. Although, I have not personally met Vanessa, my interactions with my other siblings have regrettably been less than positive.

A brief period of amicable relations existed with Kenneth and Cecil when they visited me in Kingston. During our meeting, we acknowledged our shared paternity and were content to reconnect as siblings. However, upon sharing this information with their mother, she vehemently opposed the idea, adamantly denying my status as Ronald's child and encouraging them to sever ties with me. This unfortunate incident strained the potential for a harmonious relationship among us.

I didn't really know my father until I became an adult and reached out to him. My earliest memory of him is when I was about seven years old. Salethy, sent me to his house to ask for money because we didn't have any food at the time.

Approaching his house, I saw this tall and big man who, as a small child, seemed quite intimidating. I was scared and shy, when I told him that my grandmother sent me to ask for money. He recognized me as Betsy's child and threw a $2 note down to me from the verandah, which had about six steps down to where I stood. Holding the note with the face of Paul Bogle, I hurried home and gave it to Salethy.

After sharing my experience and how insignificant I felt, Salethy promised not to send me to his house again.

I didn't interact with him for years until I met him at an Annual Community Center fair. He called me into his car and started asking me questions about myself, my school grades, and my mother. Nervously, I sat beside him and answered his questions anxiously but honestly.

As an adult, reaching out to my father allowed us to build many positive memories together. During this time, I gained insights into his thoughts and the reasons behind some of his actions. Understanding the complexities of his life, I could appreciate the challenges that he faced and the choices he made. This connection brought a newfound appreciation for the intricacies of his journey and strengthened our bond through shared understanding.

My father, a dedicated worker at the Urban Development Corporation in Kingston, often visited me during my time at the Scientific Research Council. Proudly, I introduced him to my co-workers, who were captivated by his eloquence. His manner of speaking resembled a captivating lecture, a trait perhaps inherited from his later years when he became a pastor at the Moravian Anglican Church in Manchester. I would eagerly listen to his radio sermons on Sunday mornings, basking in the pride of being his daughter.

Our conversations were not merely brief exchanges but extensive and enlightening dialogues. I gleaned a wealth of knowledge and wisdom from him. Although I regretted not having the chance to share my childhood with him, I cherished every moment we spent together. His presence was a source of immense pride, and the connection we shared as father and daughter strengthened with each passing day.

The news of his passing reached me through Auntie Sylvie, bringing forth a mix of emotions. While I mourned the missed opportunity to be by his side in his final years, I also celebrated the time we had together. In those last years, his ability to communicate over the phone dwindled, and he struggled to recognize me, yet our bond remained unbroken. Although I couldn't attend his funeral, my prayers were fervently sent to the Heavenly Father, wishing for his soul to find eternal peace.

CHAPTER EIGHT
BAUXITE AND WHITE CREPES: AUNTIE SYLVIE'S BACK-TO-SCHOOL CHRONICLES

Auntie Sylvie is my mother's big sister and first child for George Clarke and Salethy. She was also our caregiver, during Salethy's absence and would ensure that we were properly put together for school. At the beginning of the school year, she would ensure that our uniforms were neat, and we wore shoes to give a good impression on the first day of the school year. My mother, whom I called Auntie Betsy at the time, would send a white crepe for me. The crepe was like a converse sneaker with white laces. I would wear it to school immaculately white and pretty for the first couple weeks then Salethy would let me wash it with brown cake soap to take off the red mud. We would also buy whitening, which was sold in a bottle, to polish my crepe. Manchester is known for its rich red dirt, which is used to make bauxite. Bauxite is a rock formed from a reddish clay material and is used to make aluminum. Due to the rich red mud in Lancaster the Bauxite Company offered to buy out most of the lands for production, but my auntie Sylvie refused to sell her land. She did not want to relocate and root up her life. Several people in the district have accepted the offer and relocated to other areas in the nearby districts.

The quarter acre of land that I grew up on is still there, however, our neighbor sold their land to Bauxite and on my last visit I noticed that they have taken a large portion of our land as well. The part where the family plot is located was not so close to my neighbor Ms. Amy at the time when I was growing up. I can recall how we used to play on the tombs in the family plot. I also recalled that there was a tiny tomb in the plot; I later learned that it was the grave of Salethy's last child with Mass Will. We had so much fun playing on the tombs and eating the fruits from the nearby trees, which somehow were more flourishing than the other fruit trees.

We were never afraid to play in the family plot, but one day when I was a small girl, I went to a graveyard with Auntie Sylvie as one of her friends had passed. When I saw the wooden casket in one corner of the house. I was so terrified that I sat in another area and did not move for the remainder of the visit. I sat scared and prayed that Auntie Sylvie would hurry her visit and let us go home. To my surprise, we were there for the entire night as the people sang and drank coffee and white rum. It was customary at that time to visit the homes of persons who died and provide support to the grieving family. It is also customary for people to visit the graveyard every night until the ninth day, when they hold a big celebration which they called "nine nights." In those days, there were no parlors, so the bodies of deceased persons were embalmed with salt, Frankincense, myrrh and packed with dry ice until the day of the funeral. They would also remain in the house and sometimes the same room with the other family members.

One summer holiday, Auntie Sylvie took Danny, Tony, and me to an area near her house where we had to weed the grass with our hands. Her son Theophilus would dig small holes and each of us had two paint pans. One with corn and the other with red peas. Each of us was assigned a row and our task was to put three grains of corn in each hole on one side and the same for the peas on the other side.

It was a scorching summer day, and the grass was very itchy, so I wanted to finish quickly and got the idea that I could put one hand full of peas instead of the three grains as I would finish quicker. To my dismay when the peas were to be harvested my side did not flourish, because the holes were too crowded, and the peas did not have enough space to spread. My secret was revealed, and I had to pay the usual penalty of a thrashing for my actions.

During mango season Auntie Silvie took us to Quin Town mango walk to pick mangoes.

As we ventured into the mango walk, the air carried the sweet scent of ripe mangoes, and the trees adorned themselves with the vibrant kinds of their tempting fruits. Amidst this fruity haven, my favorite mango, fondly known as number 11, beckoned from the branches, promising a burst of succulent sweetness. While other mango walks boasted an array of delicious varieties, including Julie, East Indians, and sweetie come brush mi, our site was adorned with the familiarity of common mangoes, number 11, blackie, and beefy.

The act of picking mangoes from the branches became a joyous affair, with laughter and camaraderie echoing through the orchard. The experience was more than a simple harvest; it was a communion with nature, a tradition that connected us to the land and its offerings. The mango walk in Quin Town, with its limited but delectable selection, transformed into a sanctuary of flavors, textures, and shared moments, etching itself as a cherished chapter in the tapestry of our lives.

During one poignant incident that remains etched in my memory, I experienced an overwhelming sense of love. Typically, when Salethy needed to visit the hospital, I would stay with Auntie Sylvie. On a particular night, engrossed in play with my cousins Tony and Theophilus, I took a fall onto the bed panel, crafted from iron, resulting in a significant injury. At the time, I was approximately eight or nine years old and had never encountered such a profusion of blood.

In the absence of Auntie Sylvie that night, I grappled with worry, anticipating a reprimand for what I perceived as misbehavior leading to self-inflicted harm. However, Auntie Sylvie's response proved to be an unexpected showering of care and concern. The next day, she promptly took me to see a doctor and even sent a telegram to my mother in Kingston, alerting her to the severity of my injury.

Regrettably, my mother, preoccupied and perhaps unaware of the gravity of the situation, did not accord much attention to the message. Her absence during this challenging period further underscored the complexities of our relationship and the emotional dynamics, which shaped our connection.

Dandelion Dreams: *Tale of a Little Girl from Lancaster*

When Salethy returned from the hospital and found out what had happened to me, she was sorry for me, and even though she had undergone surgery herself, the sympathy and love that she showed me was unbelievable. She vowed that when I am in her care, she would do everything in her powers to keep me safe. I never felt so close to anyone before, it was magical; the love that Salethy and I shared.

I express my heartfelt gratitude to my mother for bestowing upon me the privilege of being under my grandmother's guidance. Through this entrusted responsibility, my character and moral compass were thoughtfully and diligently cultivated.

CHAPTER NINE
"COOLIE GAL' AND THE MYSTERIOUS SOUNDS OF LANCASTER"

I also recalled while growing up in Lancaster that there was a lady whom we called 'Mada, 'or 'Coolie gal.' She was a gifted psychic lady, who lived alone and wore long dresses and wrapped her head with the bandana material with a pencil stuck inside the head tie. She had drums made from goat skins and she would beat the drums and shout out serious warnings from time to time. Many people from the district thought that she was an Obeah woman, because most of her predictions were correct. I was so afraid of that lady. I would not go anywhere near her home and when she started her revival chants and warning I would run to Salethy where I felt safe.

Even though we were afraid of her, my brother Danny, cousin Tony and I, once visited her yard which looked like a barnyard. When we entered the yard, she greeted us at the gate, and we had to turn our roll (spin around) before entering. She had beautiful flowers all over the yard and ornaments of gold, drums made from goat skins and containers of different oils that she would use to anoint us. People in the district visit her when they are sick for healing. She would use her oils to anoint them and spin them around. At the beginning of each year when people go to watch night service, Mada always has service where she anoints people with holy oil and water which should give them prosperity throughout the year. Mada was not an obeah woman, she would not cast a spell on anyone, but she had the gift of discerning and could predict things before it happen and warn about them.

I recall my first encounter with an obeah woman. A real obeah woman. While I was working at the University Hospital of the West Indies my good friend Pearlie Amanda Esteen asked me to accompany her somewhere. She did not disclose where we were going but we ended up in a yard on Waltham Park Rd. As we entered the yard, I saw this lady who reminded me of Mada with her head wrapped and rope tied around her long white dress. She asked us to walk around a concrete circle, where she planted flowers. We had to turn our roll before we could go inside the house. Miss Esteen went in first and came out very somber.

When I went inside, I noticed that she had a glass of water and several candles burnt and shaped in images. She told me to put forty cents in the glass of water and five dollars on the table. I did what she told me, and she began to tell me things about myself. She told me that I was married to a government man, I was having problems with family, but my trials would soon be over. She said that I worked in an office and people were jealous of me. She also told me that I had rheumatism. I was trembling and weak in the knees, when I walked out of her house that day. I never told Miss Esteen what she told me, neither did she, but as soon as I went back to work at the hospital, I headed to the casualty department to see a doctor. I asked him how I would know if I had rheumatism. I cannot forget his laughter and the look on his face when I told him my reason for asking. The Obeah woman also conveyed to me that I possessed the gift of selling, suggesting that if I were to pursue a career as a salesperson, financial success would be within reach.

My mother rented a house on Marley Drive off Molynes Rd, and we had an interesting neighbor— an obeah lady. Over the fence, I observed a steady stream of people visiting her. She'd dress them in a black coat, instruct them to stoop down in her backyard, and then break a beer bottle over them. It was amusing to see how many people believed in her tricks.

Brady, my mother's husband, was a frequent visitor to her "balm yard." She would bathe him in pigeon blood and even gifted him a guard ring. When he later migrated to America, my sister and I discovered his guard ring, and couldn't resist peeking inside to see what was guarding him. To our surprise, we found a plastic wrapper with a dry leaf inside. We couldn't help but laugh at the irony of a man confidently wearing a guard ring that turned out to be nothing more than plastic with a dry leaf. It goes to show how belief can be powerful, even when the reality is quite different.

I vividly recall a night during my marriage to Robert, while we resided in Cooreville Gardens. He came home with two large candles, and when I inquired about them, he explained that they were for the "cleansing of the spirit." According to him, our house needed spiritual cleansing due to perceived destruction within its walls.

As Robert chanted and lit the candles, he repeated verses like "The Lord is my shepherd, I shall not want" and emphasized the need for cleansing, citing an excess of "saltness" in the house. I was left speechless, struggling to comprehend Robert's sudden involvement in such rituals. Later, he confessed to consulting an Obeah lady for spiritual guidance. It dawned on me that this was the same woman who had previously told me that I had rheumatism.

The encounter left me bewildered, prompting me to ponder the decisions and influences shaping our lives during that period. Robert used up all the salt from the kitchen cupboard, scattering it around the house in an attempt to ward off crosses and what he perceived as excess "saltness." I couldn't help but notice the irony of the situation.

In any case, the experience reinforced a lesson: never trust an obeah woman. Brady, my mother's husband, placed his faith in an obeah woman who gathered information about us simply by being our neighbor. He believed her to be a credible obeah woman based on her knowledge of our lives, highlighting the risks of relying on such practices.

CHAPTER TEN

"A SILENT STRUGGLE: SALETHY'S FIGHT AGAINST BREAST CANCER REVEALED"

Salethy was an avid smoker; she smoked tobacco in a wooden pipe like her mother Muma. As children we usually mimicked her and smoked cho cho leaf from the garden wrapped in paper. Salethy became ill when I was still at Frankfield school. She found a lump in her breast and went to a private physician in Newport about fourteen miles from Lancaster. Salethy would walk the fourteen miles from Lancaster to the doctor and back. He diagnosed her with breast cancer and to our amazement he operated on her in his office to remove the lump. Aunty Sylvie stayed at the doctor's office with her and took her home after the surgery. She recovered and was well again to continue her day-to-day activities. She became sick again and the doctor admitted her to the Mandeville Hospital. She was transferred to the Kingston Public Hospital as the cancer spread and they removed both breasts. She fought a lengthy battle with cancer. Nurses from the Red Cross would visit her and provide a care package with food for her. We were happy when the nurse visited her because we would get a wider variety of food.

As Salethy's health declined, and her strength waned, our family dynamics underwent a shift. While Danny was living with Mr. Meikle, he took up employment at his shop. It was a practical move, considering the familial ties that connected Danny to Mr. Meikle – Danny's father, Aubrey McIntyre, is the brother of Ms. Val, who is married to Mr. Meikle. This familial network further extended to Bev, as Mr. Meikle is her grandfather.

Meanwhile, Tony found himself relocated to live with his father in Clarendon. Consequently, I became the sole companion and caretaker for Salethy during her ailing days. The responsibility mirrored the care and love she had bestowed upon me throughout my upbringing. My commitment to her continued until the time came for me to leave Lancaster and join my mother in Kingston. This chapter marked an emotional period of transition and change, as the family navigated the complexities of illness and the inevitable evolution of individual paths.

Following my departure from Lancaster, Auntie Janie made a compassionate decision to send her stepdaughter, Karen, to live with Salethy. Karen's deep affection for Salethy was evident in the devoted care she provided during Salethy's moments of illness. Though I later learned that Karen, too, succumbed to cancer, her genuine kindness and warm-hearted nature left a lasting impression. I felt a sense of gratitude knowing that Karen was there for Salethy, when I could not be.

On a Saturday evening in 1977, the news of Sir Alexander Bustamante's passing echoed through the airwaves. Shortly after, my brother Danny arrived at our house with the somber news of Salethy's demise. At that time, I was residing in Washington Gardens with my mother, Brady, Bev, Sheryl, and Brady's daughter Judy, and happened to be alone, when I received the heartbreaking news.

This marked the first occasion in my life where the pain of losing a loved one hit me profoundly. A whirlwind of emotions engulfed me—grief, guilt, and profound sadness. The weight of not being with Salethy in her final moments and not having the chance to bid her farewell intensified the sorrow. The loss was especially poignant because I yearned to see her once more, to embrace her, and express my gratitude for the love and care she had showered upon me.

Salethy, my unwavering supporter and encourager, had been my biggest cheerleader, always toasting to my success and challenging me to strive for the best version of myself. During holidays, our visits were precious moments, whether in Lancaster or Kingston. The realization of her absence hit me most intensely at night, triggering a flood of memories, where she selflessly stood by me.

Despite the emotional turmoil, life demanded that I cope with school lessons and navigate the mourning process while endeavoring to excel in my studies. The challenge was formidable, yet I pressed on, driven by the memory of Salethy's enduring love and the lessons she imparted to me.

PART TWO

CHAPTER ELEVEN
CHANGING HORIZONS:
MIGRATION TO KINGSTON

The moment I bid farewell to Salethy; my entire world underwent a profound transformation. Suddenly burdened with the responsibility of caring for my younger sister, Sheryl, my life took an unforeseen turn, and the prospect of attending school became an unattainable luxury. With no one else available to babysit Sheryl, while our mother worked, I assumed the role of her caregiver, forfeiting my own educational pursuits.

Leaving Lancaster and the familiar halls of Frankfield School marked the beginning of a significant hiatus in my academic journey. It was not until the eighth grade that I found myself back within the walls of a classroom. The intervening years, spanning from grade four to seven, became an unintended gap in my education, a period during which I missed crucial learning milestones and the opportunity to sit examinations for placement in a government high school. The responsibility of babysitting my younger sister was entrusted to me, a duty that required my careful attention and nurturing care. As the designated caregiver, at age eleven I took on the role of ensuring her safety, comfort, and well-being during the times, when our mother was away. This duty not only fostered a sense of responsibility within me but also deepened the bond between my sister and me as we navigated the challenges and joys of growing up together.

Sheryl's father was Charles Ferguson, a gentleman fondly referred to as 'Daddy 'by everyone at the time. I have vivid memories of him owning a white scooter bike, adding a touch of charm to his visits. During the daytime, he would drop by, engaging warmly with us. However, come nightfall, he had to return to his home and wife, Ms. Dottie.

Our shared address, 15 Texton Rd, represented a sizable tenement yard, housing two distinct residences on the property. My mother occupied a single room in the yard at first, and later, we relocated to the other side of the house, boasting an expansive verandah shared with Mrs. Hamilton. In hindsight, it amuses me to recall the weekly ritual of cleaning our half of the verandah with red floor polish every Saturday. The remaining responsibility for the other half rested on the shoulders of fellow tenants, Miss Winnie, and Mother Hamilton.

The outcome of this communal effort varied, creating amusing scenarios, where our portion would gleam with red genie polish while the other half remained untouched. These recollections weave together the fabric of our communal living, marked by shared responsibilities, and the unique dynamics that unfolded within the community.

Amidst these shared spaces, a vivid memory emerges of Mother Hamilton's daughter, Jean. Despite her slender physique, she carried an aura that made her seem like a big girl compared to my skinny frame at the time. But because Jean looked like a young lady older men would make advances at her.

One of my mother's cousins, a policeman at the time, took a keen interest in Jean, often visiting when our mothers were at work and Jean was home from school. He even picked her up from school some of the time and abused her before dropping her home.

Mr. and Mrs. Benjie, residing at 32 Rousseau Rd, were our neighbors with a grocery shop where we purchased our essentials. They were blessed with about six children, with Una being the eldest. The yard was always bustling with activity as all the children, including Una, would gather to watch Dark Shadows together from outside the window of Sonia and Winston's apartment, who was affectionately known as 'James Bond'.

Those were joyful times with plenty of children growing up in the spacious yard. I distinctly recall a day, when Mrs. Benjie lost some money. In an attempt to uncover the culprit, she brought a Bible and a key to our house. The method involved placing a house key within the Bible and calling out names. According to the belief, when the name of the thief was called, the Bible would vibrate. We eagerly gathered around, awaiting the revelation, but as expected, the Bible remained still – a testament to the playful myths that added charm to our childhood memories.

In 1976, Daddy endured a stroke that rendered him unable to visit Mother. He resided with his wife, Ms. Dottie, at 52 Arnold Rd, and Mother, unable to make the trip to see him, sent me in her stead one day to check on his well-being. During our brief encounter, he inquired about Mother and Sheryl, expressing concern for their welfare. However, as time passed and we relocated to Washington Gardens, we received no further updates about Daddy, including the circumstances of his eventual passing. The silence surrounding his fate left a lingering sense of mystery and detachment.

I left Frankfield Primary School during my fourth-grade year, marking a temporary gap in my academic journey. It wasn't until Aunt Minna, Salethy's sister, assumed the role of caregiver for my sister Sheryl that I had the opportunity to resume my education.

I was enrolled in St. Anne's Junior Secondary School, where my brother also attended, I found myself placed in grade 8A – considered the top tier among grade 8s. This designation was not due to completing all the primary grades but rather based on my age. Although, there was a gap in my primary education, I managed to catch up, performing at an average level and securing promotion to the ninth grade.

Regrettably, circumstances prevented me from sitting the government examinations that would have determined placement in secondary schools. Leaving Frankfield Primary before reaching grades five or six meant missing the Common Entrance Examination. This decision was primarily driven by the need to care for Sheryl in the absence of alternative arrangements. Additionally, I couldn't take the 9th Grade Achievement test to secure a spot in the third form of Government Secondary High schools due to the simultaneous upgrade of Junior Secondary Schools to the

Secondary level in the same year, I reached grade 9. These challenges shaped my educational path, emphasizing the importance of adapting to circumstances beyond my control.

Mrs. Brissett, serving as the Vice Principal of St Anne's Junior Secondary School during that time, played a pivotal role in shaping my educational journey. She became a beacon of inspiration, consistently drawing out the best in me. We affectionately referred to her as 'Mother,' a term that reflected the deep fondness she had for me. Mrs. Brissett took me under her wings, fostering a nurturing environment that extended beyond academics.

In her encouragement, I took the step to embrace Catholicism, a decision that marked significant milestones such as confirmation and my first communion, both of which occurred during my time at school. Thursday afternoons were dedicated to confessing our sins to the priest. However, I harbored a secret – every Thursday, I would weave tales to avoid disclosing that I spent afterschool hours in a shop with my friends, Karlene, Beverly, and Norma. We formed a close-knit group known as the "Fabulous Four."

During confession, I would admit to disobedience toward my mother and confess to stealing sugar. The repetition of this confession became a ritual, with the priest guiding me through prayers to seek forgiveness. The routine, while not entirely truthful, highlighted the complexities of adolescence and the camaraderie forged with friends during those formative years.

Visiting Mrs. Brissett's home on St James Ave became a cherished routine for me, deepening the bond between us. Our connection extended to her daughter Sharon, with whom I formed a lasting friendship. Together, we attended St. Elizabeth Catholic Church on Ransford Avenue, sharing moments of faith and community.

During Christmas programs, Mrs. Brissett ensured my active participation, fostering a sense of inclusion and joy. I vividly recall one memorable Christmas when I portrayed an angel, receiving dance lessons from the instructor at St Anne's. The anticipation of performing on stage in front of a large audience filled me with excitement. Overwhelmed with joy as I spotted my mother and sister in the audience, enthusiastically cheering me on.

Our involvement extended beyond school events; we had the privilege of performing at the grand gala at the National Stadium and participating in the Float parade during Independence celebrations. Mrs. Brissett's leadership extended to the Red Cross Club at St Anne's, an invitation she extended to me. Through this club, we volunteered at the Kingston Public Hospital, where we would read to patients.

Additionally, on Saturdays, a group of us would visit the Glen Vincent Home, contributing our time to assist in the kitchen or engage in cleaning duties. Mrs. Brissett's guidance went beyond extracurricular activities; she consistently encouraged me to carry myself with pride and to make both my mother and her proud. Her mentorship left an indelible mark, shaping not just my academic experiences, but also instilling a sense of responsibility and compassion.

CHAPTER TWELVE
NAVAGATING EDUCATIONAL TRANSITIONS: SIBLING SUPPORT

Upon completing the 9th Grade at St Anne's, I heeded Mrs. Brissett's guidance and took the initiative to sit an entrance examination for St Hugh's High for Girls. When I shared this decision with my mother, it triggered a wave of anger. She was displeased with the prospect of me attending the Extension school, characterized as "Evening Class," as it meant that I would be on the road after 6 pm.

In response to my mother's concerns, she enrolled me in Kingsway High School, a private Adventist school, where I spent four years, spanning grades 8 through 11. Despite having completed the ninth grade at St Anne's, my entrance examination results placed me in the 8th grade.

During this period, my sister Sheryl began her schooling journey at Rousseau Primary, situated off Maxfield Avenue and Rousseau Rd. Every morning, I would take her to school and then make my way back to Kencot for my classes. In the evenings, after my school day concluded, I would pick her up from Veronica Morgan's house. (Auntie Dye.) Auntie Dye, a teacher at Rousseau Primary, was married to my uncle Babba. The journey from Kencot to Lyndhurst Rd to retrieve my sister was a routine, and together we would travel back home to Texton Rd. On occasions when our brother Danny, employed at Georgie Girl Shoe store in Cross Road, was available, he would also assist in picking her up from school.

My sister was very precocious and excelled at Rousseau Primary School. By the time, she reached grade 2, she was reading encyclopedias and could recite long and difficult poems from memory. She would accompany me to Church of the Open Bible, on Washington Gardens, where I was a member and would always offer the welcome, whenever we had Christmas Programs. She was successful in the Common Entrance Examinations and placed at the Queens School, which was her first choice.

My high school years were challenging. I could not balance my role of caring for my sister and studying. God in His Mercy pulled me through, and I completed my studies and graduated with my high school diploma. I was successful in the General Certificate of Examinations, which qualified me to attend college. The morning after graduation my father came to congratulate me and expressed how proud he was of me. In those days, many girls did not successfully complete high school, so he was indeed proud. He offered to pay for my college. I had two options at the time: to go to Teachers 'or Secretarial College. I opted for Secretarial and enrolled in Fitz Henley's Secretarial College where I studied, Business Education and stenography.

My father also asked one of his friends, Mr. Mossop, to give me a summer job at the Mossop Construction on Maxfield Ave.

I left Fitz Henley's College and went to work at the University Hospital of the West Indies. My first job was as a Stenographer at the School of Nursing. It was there, I met my good friends Janet McBean, Pearlie Esteen, Ann Marie Walker, Rosemarie Scully, Rosie and Joan Williams, whom I am friends with to this day. Joan and I went to college and reunited at the University Hospital. My sister accompanied me to work at the University Hospital of the West Indies one summer and she was well loved by all my co-workers who were appalled by her level of intelligence at such an early age.

CHAPTER THIRTEEN
"EMBRACING LOVE: FROM CHANCE MEETINGS TO LASTING BONDS"

One fine morning at the School of Nursing, a handsome electrical technician approached me with a purchase requisition for a faulty wire in one of the classrooms. Engrossed in my typing, I requested a moment to complete my sentence, a task that required precision on the non-forgiving typewriter. Unimpressed, the technician grew impatient, and I eventually showed him to the classroom.

Upon inspection, he inquired about additional issues with the wire, to which I responded with the details specified in the requisition. After answering his questions, I politely asked, if I could leave, but his dismissive reply hinted at his frustration. Undeterred, I returned to my typing. When he finished the job, he informed me and left.

Days later, he returned with another purchase order, and although, I hadn't initiated the request, I led him to the designated area. This time, he sought information about me, my name and origin. Uninterested in his inquiries, I hurriedly left after guiding him to the room.

To my surprise, my office mate informed me that the technician had been looking for me. Intrigued, I pondered his intentions. Upon his return, he sought assurance that his work met my satisfaction. Modestly, I confirmed its adequacy, noting the absence of complaints from the tutor who used the classroom. Soon after, as I prepared for lunch, he reappeared, inquiring about my lunch destination. I mentioned the Pathology canteen, and although, I usually lunched with friends, he expressed interest in joining. However, when we returned to the school together, it became apparent that his presence was more than coincidental. As we walked in silence, he bid me goodbye upon reaching my office.

This unexpected sequence of encounters left me intrigued and questioning his motives, creating a subtle yet intriguing connection in the unassuming environment of the School of Nursing. He persisted in his visits, diligently warding off any potential suitors who might vie for my attention. Over time, our connection deepened, evolving into a blossoming relationship that transcended the boundaries of mere friendship.

After four years of courtship, we decided to embark on a new chapter of our journey. A journey adorned with love and sealed our commitment on a rainy Saturday afternoon. The Church of the Open Bible, a place where my heart had found its sanctuary, became the ethereal setting for our union. Our reception unfolded at the Jamaica Defense Force, Up Park Camp, a place close to our hearts as it held the memories of my husband's service in the First Battalion. It became the perfect backdrop for a celebration filled with love, joy, and happiness, surrounded by cherished family and friends.

The tables were simple yet adorned with bursts of color, creating a lively, and welcoming atmosphere. The air was filled with the delicious aroma of a feast, symbolizing not just the union of two souls but the beautiful fusion of our two worlds.

As we embraced the dance floor, the gentle rain outside provided a rhythmic accompaniment to the melody of our shared joy. It was a moment of pure bliss, surrounded by the people we love and the simple yet profound beauty of our union.

Our matrimonial home at 55 Wailers Avenue in Cooreville Gardens, Kingston, Jamaica, was a place brimming with cherished memories for me. It was not just a house but a haven where I crossed paths with many wonderful souls. As the saying goes, "it takes a village to raise a child," I am eternally grateful for the village that surrounded us.

Mrs. Barnett, the McLeans, Miss G, Charm, and Mrs. Campbell were more than neighbors; they became pillars of support in the upbringing of my two children. Their kindness, guidance, and invaluable contributions formed an integral part of our family tapestry. Each name is etched in the heartwarming story of our home, creating a sense of community that made 55 Wailers Avenue not just an address, but a place filled with the warmth of shared experiences and neighborly love.

During that time, my sister was living with us, and the challenges that we faced were unimaginable. As a teenager on the brink of adulthood, she grappled with the complexities of adolescence, all the while harboring the anticipation of soon moving to America. Although younger than me, she sought independence and occasionally faced challenges that put our family bonds to the test.

Dandelion Dreams: *Tale of a Little Girl from Lancaster*

During a challenging situation of separation from her mother at this pivotal time, I recognized the importance of addressing the underlying issues and providing her with the support she needed to navigate through difficult times. I took the initiative to arrange a meeting with a counselor from the University Hospital of the West Indies. Understanding the sensitivity of the situation, I maintained discretion about the specific details, simply alluding to a meeting with a doctor. This meeting, which took place in the Psychiatric Department at the University Hospital, provided an opportunity to explore and understand the root causes of my sister's disruptive behavior. She expressed reluctance regarding the prospect of meeting with a doctor from the Psychiatry department and declined to engage in conversation with the physician. Consequently, the endeavor proved unsuccessful.

During this challenging period, I grappled with feelings of powerlessness. I came to understand that her actions were likely a response to the absence of our mother and the financial struggles we were facing. Despite these difficulties, I held onto the belief in my sister's inherent brilliance and determination.

Recognizing her potential for success, I remained optimistic about her future. I understood that the toll of not having her mother around during such a pivotal time had impacted her, but I had faith in her resilience. With her determination and academic prowess, I was confident that she would bounce back and achieve the success she was destined for. During this challenging period, my prayers focused on her safety and well-being, knowing that she had the strength to overcome adversity and emerge triumphant.

Finding solace after several years, Mother eventually took Sheryl to the United States to live with her. This marked the conclusion of a deeply challenging chapter in my life, and I felt a profound sense of relief and gratitude. Sheryl, thrilled at the opportunity, embraced her new life in the United States, pursuing a successful career in the United States Navy. Today, she stands as a proud wife and mother of three boys, embodying a life that has taken a positive and fulfilling turn.

I couldn't be prouder of the incredible woman Sheryl has become. Our shared journey, from the challenges of childhood to the triumphs of adulthood, has strengthened our bond as sisters. The adversities we faced together only served to deepen our connection, and I am thankful for the growth, resilience, and joy that define Sheryl's life today.

The weight of heartbreak, depression, hurt, and anger became overwhelming as I navigated life in Cooreville Gardens. The emotional turmoil intensified as the people I loved seemed to turn against me, leaving me grappling with a sense of powerlessness in the face of circumstances beyond my control.

Confronted with a tumultuous marriage marked by my husband's consistent absence, justified by his purported army duties, our financial difficulties escalated. The strain intensified with the added challenges of infidelity and disrespect, prompting me to make a critical decision to reclaim my sense of self.

In second grade at Frankfield Primary School, I distinctly recall a significant moment when Miss Combs' class was to be assessed for reading by Principal Mr. Gooden, I eagerly volunteered to be the first reader, fueled by confidence in my reading abilities. However, when he posed a question about the material I just read, nervousness overwhelmed me, preventing a response.

Despite the setback, I resolved to rectify the situation. I joined another group, and Mr. Gooden posed four questions, assuring full marks for correct answers. With unwavering determination, I provided correct responses, prompting him to amend my score. In recognition of my efforts, he allowed me to select a book from the library to take home and read.

This experience taught me a valuable lesson about the power of choice. Recognizing that I had the choice to accept the first score influenced by nerves or to redeem myself and achieve a better outcome. It became an essential moment in understanding that I could shape my own path through the choices that I made.

Applying a similar approach in my marriage, I made the conscious decision not to be confined by the past but to evolve into a better version of myself. Prioritizing my peace of mind, I recognized the significance of preserving my sanity, leading me to choose the path of walking away. The sentiments expressed in Bruce Springsteen's "Streets of Philadelphia," where he writes, "I was bruised and battered. I could not tell what I felt, I saw my reflection in the window and did not even know my own face," resonated deeply with my emotions during my time as a soldier's wife at 55 Wailers Avenue.

Robert was undeniably handsome, earning the endearing nickname 'pretty Paul' from his counterparts in the Jamaica Defense Force. He used his good looks to charm and easily attract the attention of unsuspecting women.

The abundance of affection that he received from women might have influenced him negatively, causing disruptive behavior and a lack of respect toward me as his wife. Despite Launa his sister's encouragement for him to show respect to his family, he became careless and started sharing our home phone number with various women. This led to a barrage of calls, turning into a source of harassment for me.

Whenever I raised concerns about the calls, it sadly escalated into instances of physical violence.

The lesson I learned from that experience is not to engage in a conflict unless I am prepared for the potential consequences. Despite the challenges in our marriage, we also shared some memorable moments. I fondly remember one Sunday, when we cooked a pot of rice and peas with chicken, embarking on a road trip to explore the entire island of Jamaica, stopping at each major town along the way.

On a particular Sunday, after spending the weekend with his parents and on our way back home, we got into an argument. He abruptly left Annalise, Bobby, and me on the roadside, and we had to find our own way back home. Despite his fun-loving nature, there were times when Robert lacked judgment and administered harsh punishments.

In reflecting on our past, I have chosen to portray my ex-husband as a figure who played a significant role in our shared experiences. This narrative captures moments of both; joy and challenges, encapsulating the complexities of our relationship. It is a sincere account of our journey together.

I made a conscious decision to refrain from dwelling on the adversities, instead, I chose to concentrate on the positive aspects. The journey I have undertaken has been transformative, and the lessons learned have played a significant role in shaping the person I am today.

In 2001, we left from Cooreville Gardens, and around the same time, Robert left for the United States. I felt a sense of joy, when he called for a family meeting and declared his intention to go to the States. I vividly remember ironing his clothes on a broken ironing board, with Annalise having to hold it up, and packing his suitcase for his departure.

Upon Robert's invitation, I made a trip to the United States to visit him during the period when he resided in Lauderhill. It was during this visit that I discerned, with a sense of disappointment, that he continued to traverse the same path of infidelity that had been a source of concern. Despite the change in geographic location, there was a conspicuous lack of transformation in his behavior, reinforcing my realization that the geographical relocation had not induced the anticipated shift in his conduct. This realization served as a pivotal moment, crystallizing my decision to bid a final farewell. In retrospect, I acknowledge that my initial optimism, hoping for a positive change linked to his altered environment, was perhaps a misguided expectation. Following that, we concluded our divorce proceedings in the year 2002.

CHAPTER FOURTEEN
"THROUGH TRIALS AND TRIUMPHS: A MOTHER'S JOURNEY OF LOVE AND RESILIENCE"

February 11, 1987, etched itself into the fabric of my memories as an unforgettable day, marked by the arrival of my firstborn, whom I lovingly named Annalise Roxanne Smith. The preceding day, February 10, 1987, echoed with the somber news of Edna Manley's passing, a moment imprinted in my mind as I reclined on the couch in my Cooreville Gardens home, engaged in conversation with my mother.

In the quietude of that evening, a sudden, sharp pain pierced through my belly, signaling the onset of labor. In that moment, a prayer emerged from the depths of my being, beseeching the Divine for strength, and a reminder that the pain, I endured was transient, destined to culminate in the joy of welcoming a precious life. Terrified and uncertain of what lay ahead, I embarked on an 18-hour journey of labor, marked by the endurance of pain and the anticipation of the new chapter about to unfold.

After enduring the challenges of labor and undergoing an episiotomy, the culmination of this arduous journey arrived—a moment of unparalleled joy as I cradled my newborn in my arms. The mantle of motherhood draped itself around me, signaling a profound shift in the landscape of my existence. No longer was my life solely my own; it now intertwined with the delicate responsibility of nurturing a tiny human destined to evolve into a wholesome adult, poised to make meaningful contributions to society.

In the sacred act of becoming a mother, I embraced a divine charge, echoing the words of Genesis 1:28, "Be fruitful, and multiply, and replenish the earth, and subdue it: and have dominion over the fish of the sea, and over the fowl of the air, and over every living thing that moveth upon the earth." This scripture reverberated through the chambers of my heart, underscoring the sacred duty entrusted to me—to guide, nurture, and instill values in the precious life, I had brought into the world. From that day forward, the tapestry of my life intertwined with that of my child, embarking on a shared journey of growth, love, and the promise of a future filled with infinite possibilities.

Steeped in the profound love and enduring values that Salethy showered upon me, I was resolute in bestowing the same boundless affection and attention upon my precious daughter. Every ounce of my being was devoted to her, and the invaluable lessons Salethy imparted echoed in my mind as I tenderly nurtured this little soul.

Annalise's unwavering dedication to success became unmistakably evident during her tenure at King's Gate Preparatory School. Her relentless pursuit of excellence not only garnered her numerous awards but also filled our hearts with pride.

When she started high school at Immaculate Conception, she invited her classmates over to our home for sleepovers and study sessions. Witnessing the camaraderie and dedication, I became confident in the potential of these young ladies and was certain they would achieve great heights. As time progressed, she transformed into an extraordinary young woman, adorning her journey from primary to high school with brilliance and character. Driven by the unwavering determination to afford her the opportunities that I longed for, I observed the unfurling of her innate potential and the actualization of her dreams. Her exceptional journey not only showcased individual brilliance but also set an inspiring pace for her sibling to follow. As a trailblazer in the family, she became a living example of perseverance, determination, and achievement. Her accomplishments served as a guiding light for her younger brother, illustrating that with hard work and dedication, he too could reach his aspirations. She inadvertently became a role model, fostering a culture of ambition, and excellence within the family, creating a positive ripple effect that influenced her sibling to strive for the best in his own unique ways.

Years later in the embrace of motherhood, Annalise gifted us a precious treasure. On January 28, 2018, Belay entered the world, becoming an instant source of pure joy— a tiny bundle of happiness carrying the promise of a brighter tomorrow.

His laughter and innocence brought color to our lives, turning ordinary days into extraordinary memories. With each passing moment, he painted our world with the hues of happiness and endless possibilities.

As I look back to that special day, I am reminded that life is a beautiful canvas, and my grandson is the artist who continues to add brightness to our journey. His presence is a constant reminder of the simple and profound beauty that surrounds us, making every day a celebration of love and laughter.

Today, as I stand in awe of the extraordinary woman she has become, my heart overflows with gratitude to God for these immeasurable blessings.

CHAPTER FIFTEEN

"BOBBY'S ARRIVAL: A BEACON OF LOVE AND STRENGTH IN CHALLENGING TIMES"

Bobby (Banton), a remarkable gift and my second-born, made his entrance into the world on December 15, 1988, becoming the youngest member of our family. His arrival followed closely on the heels of his elder sister, Annalise, who had graced us with her presence just one year and ten months prior.

In those challenging times marked by financial hardships, Bobby's birth brought a mix of joy and responsibility. As a member of the Jamaica Defense Force, Robert, my husband, dedicated significant time to his duties, often leaving us to navigate the complexities of life with limited familial support. Amidst these difficulties, Bobby emerged as a beacon of love and strength.

His innate sense of protection became evident early on, a trait that would later define his character. Even as a young boy, he displayed a profound love for his mother, standing as a pillar of support during times, when Robert's military commitments kept him away from home. Bobby's unique qualities, a blend of love and a natural inclination to shield his family, set the stage for the extraordinary role he would play in our lives.

Bobby, in addition to being my son, evolved into my protector and most cherished treasure. On a particular Saturday afternoon, following an altercation with my husband, Bobby went with me to his mistress 'house to address the situation.

Amidst the emotional devastation I was experiencing, all I wanted was for Robert to grant me the space I needed. However, he persisted in his provocations by incessantly calling me from her house as if to deliberately taunt and intensify my distress. In the depths of enduring a lifetime marked by abuse, I found myself on a journey filled with pain. The overwhelming desire to bring an end to this torment consumed my thoughts. That night, as Bobby held my hand, I felt a profound sense of loss and vulnerability.

Bobby's resilience and character experienced profound growth during his adolescent years, particularly when he entered an all-boys school at St Georges College and crossed paths with the remarkable Vice Principal, Ms.

Dandelion Dreams: *Tale of a Little Girl from Lancaster*

Virgo. Much like Mrs. Brissett did for me, Miss Virgo extended her nurturing wings over Bobby, playing a pivotal role in his personal and academic development.

As I contemplate the remarkable journey of my son's growth, a profound sense of pride engulfs me. Bobby, beyond his exceptional musical talents and adeptness in mathematics, stands out as a young man with a heart characterized by sweetness and abundant love. As a mother, the current tapestry of my emotions is woven with threads of joy and gratitude, witnessing the development of a truly wonderful soul in him. His multifaceted gifts and the genuine warmth within his heart are sources of immense pride and fill my maternal heart with an overwhelming sense of fulfillment and appreciation.

Bobby's emergence as a leader became unmistakably apparent during our residence on Tennyson Boulevard in Dunrobin. He confidently stepped into the role of the man of the house, fearlessly tackling responsibilities that were typically reserved for seasoned experts. He managed household tasks with remarkable efficiency, from handling complex repairs to managing our finances. In doing so, he not only showcased his natural leadership abilities but also demonstrated a maturity that exceeded his years. Bobby's resilience was evident as he navigated these challenges with unwavering determination, never shying away from the hard work required to keep our household running smoothly. His ability to remain calm under pressure and make thoughtful decisions in difficult situations underscored his exceptional capability as a leader and his profound commitment to our family's well-being.

Today, I stand proud and salute Bobby for the hard work and determination he demonstrated in acquiring his BSc in Electrical Engineering. This achievement was not without its hardships and ups and downs. Bobby faced numerous challenges along the way, from grueling study sessions and demanding projects to balancing part-time jobs and personal commitments. Despite these obstacles, he remained steadfast in his pursuit of excellence, never allowing setbacks to deter him from his goal. His resilience and unwavering focus were truly inspiring, as he continually pushed himself to overcome every hurdle that came his way. Bobby's journey is a testament to his perseverance and dedication, qualities that will undoubtedly serve him well in all his future endeavors. His success is not just a reflection of his academic prowess but also of his extraordinary character and indomitable spirit.

CHAPTER SIXTEEN

UNVEILING POTENTIAL: A JOURNEY THROUGH PROFESSIONAL GROWTH AND ACHIEVEMENT"

In 1994, I accomplished the successful completion of the Certified Professional Secretary (CPS) examinations, marking a pivotal moment in my professional journey. Eager to capitalize on this achievement, I embarked on my first professional endeavor with Alkalied Limited, a company owned by Barclay Ewart. Regrettably, my tenure there was unexpectedly brief, representing the initial instance of job termination in my career.

This posed a significant challenge, especially given the circumstances surrounding my departure. Having initially resigned and later sought to retract that resignation, I found myself facing termination months later. This experience imparted a crucial lesson, emphasizing the importance of trusting my instincts and standing by my decisions. It also highlighted the potential for tough situations to harbor hidden opportunities.

Following the termination, I briefly reflected on the experience before securing a position at the Jamaica Broadcasting Corporation (JBC) as a temporary secretary, filling in for someone on maternity leave. Working in the newsroom alongside professionals like Cliff Hughes and Faye Ellington, I gained valuable insights and exposure. Afterward, I made a career transition to the Jamaica Development Bank and subsequently to the Scientific Research Council (SRC), where I not only solidified my professional standing but also cultivated enduring professional relationships and lasting friendships. Among the individuals with whom I formed lasting connections are Denise, Oreal, and Andrea Spencer Small, with whom I still maintain regular contact. Presently, Andrea serves as my primary confidante, providing a listening ear when needed. We frequently reminisce about our shared experiences at SRC. In particular, we often laugh about an incident involving Beulah Taylor, an older lady who humorously expressed her intention to purchase a pair of shorts and invite her husband to the North Coast to reignite their relationship. Regrettably, we now recognize that our amusement at the time obscured the underlying message—

Dandelion Dreams: *Tale of a Little Girl from Lancaster*

Beulah was facing significant marital difficulties and making earnest attempts to reconcile the situation. Regrettably, our amusement at her desire to wear shorts at her age caused us to overlook her struggles. Despite the geographical distance that separates Denise and me, a lasting bond continues to connect us. While our communication may not be frequent, there exists an unspoken sense of gratitude and a resilient friendship that endures. The shared journey we experienced and the mutual support we provided to each other, along with the enduring bond between our children, are aspects that remain indelible in our memories.

Additionally, I developed a sustained friendship with Kaleb. Our connection is like a work of art, where kind words and meaningful gestures create a deep bond. These elements are not just surface level; they are threads that intertwine, making our relationship profound and lasting. Each act of kindness adds richness to our shared experiences, forming a tangible connection of understanding, and emotions that lasts.

My time at SRC was marked by a restructuring phase, leading to staff redundancies. Seizing the opportunity, I decided to visit my sister in the United States. At that time, she was residing in Key West. Coincidentally, my daughter, Annalise, had just graduated from high school and expressed a desire to pursue college education in the United States. This presented an exciting and opportune moment for our family.

PART THREE

CHAPTER SEVENTEEN
"REUNION AND RENEWAL: A JOURNEY OF SACRIFICE, AND JOY"

After Annalise graduated from high school, my sister encouraged us to start a new chapter in the United States. I took Annalise and Bobby to live with my sister in Virginia Beach. Unfortunately, due to immigration issues, I had to return to Jamaica and couldn't go back to the U.S. for almost six years. During this time, I endured three unbearable years without seeing Annalise and Bobby, relying on MSN messenger for communication. Following my departure from the U.S., Sheryl sent them to live with their father, Robert, who was in Florida at the time.

I consider myself genuinely fortunate to have crossed paths with Lloyd Miller, a dear friend of my father whose generosity and warmth left an indelible mark on my life. In an extraordinary display of kindness, Lloyd went above and beyond by graciously opening his home to me. His hospitality provided not just a roof over my head but also a haven of comfort during a transitional period in my life.

Dandelion Dreams: Tale of a Little Girl from Lancaster

Facing the challenge of being separated from my children for three years was an experience marked by profound sadness and an overwhelming sense of regret and disappointment that is difficult to articulate fully. This period of separation was a significant emotional ordeal, one that reshaped my understanding of life and relationships in ways I had never anticipated.

The sadness I felt was deep and pervasive, touching every aspect of my daily existence. The absence of my children created a void that was constantly felt, a persistent ache that reminded me of the invaluable moments we were missing. This sadness was not merely about the physical separation but also about the emotional and psychological distance that grew as time passed. It was a longing for their presence, their laughter, and the simple, yet profound, joy of being part of their lives on a daily basis.

Regret and disappointment were my constant companions during this time. There was a persistent, nagging sense of having failed in my role as a parent. I regretted the circumstances that led to our separation, and this regret often morphed into self-recrimination and guilt. The disappointment was not just with the situation but with myself, as I questioned the decisions I had made and the impact they had on my children. This self-reflection was painful and relentless, a continuous process of questioning and doubting my actions and their consequences.

Through these difficult times, I found myself reflecting deeply on life. The separation forced me to confront my vulnerabilities and weaknesses, as well as my strengths and capacities for resilience. I experienced a wide range of emotions, each contributing to a complex tapestry of feelings that defined this period. Love was a constant, even in separation; my love for my children remained steadfast and unwavering, a beacon that guided me through the darkest moments.

Kindness also emerged as a significant theme. During this time, I encountered the kindness of friends particularly Lloyd Miller whose generosity I will never forget. His support and understanding provided much-needed solace and encouragement. Such acts of kindness were reminders of the goodness in the world, even when I felt overwhelmed by sadness and regret.

However, these years were also marked by feelings of betrayal. There were moments when I felt betrayed by the circumstances that led to our separation, by systems or individuals I had trusted, and sometimes even by life itself.

This sense of betrayal compounded the emotional turmoil, adding layers of complexity to my already fraught state of mind.

Despite the emotional hardship, these years of separation were a profound period of growth and introspection. I learned to navigate my emotions with greater depth and understanding, acknowledging the mixed feelings of love, kindness, and betrayal without letting them define me. I discovered an inner strength and resilience that I had not known existed, and these traits helped me endure and ultimately move forward.

This period of separation from my children was a crucible in which my character was tested and refined. It forced me to face my deepest fears and insecurities, and in doing so, I emerged with a stronger sense of self and a renewed commitment to my children and our future together. While the experience was undeniably painful, it was also a catalyst for profound personal transformation, shaping me into a more compassionate, resilient, and reflective individual.

During a time when uncertainty loomed and I was in search of employment, Lloyd's generosity served as a beacon of hope, casting a reassuring light on my journey.

The impact of his kindness was significant, transforming what could have been a challenging period into a chapter of growth and resilience. Gratitude fills my heart as I reflect on the invaluable role Lloyd played during this pivotal time. His selfless gesture not only provided me with a place to stay but also instilled in me a profound appreciation for the power of compassion and the enduring impact of genuine human connection. I am truly thankful for the fortuitous intersection of our lives and the positive influence he had on my journey.

I secured a position at the University of the West Indies as a Faculty Representative for the Medical Sciences. It was there that I encountered remarkable individuals. Notably, Cordel Nelson's impact on my life was profound and transformative. As the Faculty Representative for Medical Sciences at the University of the West Indies, I found myself in a challenging yet rewarding position. The journey towards my current role was marked by ups and downs, but it was the unwavering support and guidance of Mr. Nelson that made a significant difference.

Dandelion Dreams: *Tale of a Little Girl from Lancaster*

From the moment I stepped into the role, Cordel Nelson's generosity and kindness became evident. Despite his enigmatic aura, he had a unique way of making those around him feel seen and valued. His leadership style was a blend of professionalism and genuine concern for the well-being of his colleagues. It was this combination that created an environment conducive to personal and professional growth.

During the initial phases of my tenure, I faced various obstacles that left me feeling overwhelmed. Mr. Nelson sensed my struggles and extended a helping hand without hesitation. Whether it was offering insightful advice, providing constructive feedback, or simply lending a sympathetic ear, he played a crucial role in helping me navigate the challenges.

Beyond the professional realm, Cordel Nelson's influence extended to the formation of lasting connections with remarkable individuals at the University. The network I built during my time there, under his leadership, continues to enrich my personal and professional life. Some of these connections have evolved into enduring friendships that have withstood the test of time.

Panseta Smith

As I reflect on my journey, I am acutely aware of the significant role Cordel Nelson played in shaping my trajectory. His passing has left a void at the University of the West Indies, and the collective mourning is a testament to the impact he had on the institution. Despite the loss, I am grateful for the legacy of support and kindness he left behind, a legacy that continues to inspire and guide me.

In honoring Cordel Nelson's memory, I am reminded of the profound influence one person can have on the lives of others. His kindness, generosity, and leadership have become an enduring source of inspiration, guiding me in both my professional and personal endeavors. Though he may be physically absent, his legacy lives on in the lives he touched, and I am forever grateful for the role he played in helping me get back on my feet.

During my tenure at the University, I was given the opportunity to take part in Examiners meetings held in Trinidad and Tobago and Barbados. It was at one of these meetings that I had the privilege of meeting Jan Joseph Lewis, an exceptional woman whose influence played a significant role in helping me acclimate to the Trinidadian culture. The news of her passing filled me with deep sadness, as she had been a welcoming and guiding presence during my time in Trinidad.

After devoting four years to the University of the West Indies, the resolution of my immigration issues marked a transformative turning point in my life. The culmination of this process allowed me to finally reunite with my children in the United States. The day Bobby came to pick me up at the airport remains etched in my memory as a moment of profound relief, symbolizing the conclusion of our prolonged separation and the commencement of a new chapter filled with immense joy. That pivotal moment not only marked the end of a challenging chapter but also heralded the beginning of a fresh and heartwarming phase in our family's journey.

As I conclude this journey that took me from the cobblestone streets of Lancaster to the vibrant halls of Kingston and eventually to the vast expanse of the United States, I am filled with a profound sense of gratitude and introspection. The path I've traveled, marked by challenges, triumphs, and unexpected encounters, has shaped me in ways I could never have imagined.

Lancaster, with its historic charm, was the starting point of my narrative – a place where the seeds of ambition were sown. Kingston, a city pulsating with the rhythm of academia and the warmth of camaraderie, became a pivotal chapter where I honed my skills and found lifelong connections. And then, the United States, a land of opportunity and diversity, offered a canvas for new experiences and growth.

As I reflect on my journey I am reminded that it is not merely about the physical places traversed but the people encountered along the way. Each person, like a character in a novel, played a role in the unfolding story of my life. From the enigmatic Cordel Nelson, who helped me find my footing, to the remarkable individuals at the University of the West Indies, and the diverse tapestry of personalities in the United States – they have all left indelible marks on the pages of my existence.

This journey has been a testament to resilience, adaptability, and the power of human connection. It has taught me that life's narrative is unpredictable, and every twist and turn contribute to the richness of my life. As I stand on the threshold of new beginnings, I carry with me the lessons learned, the friendships forged, and the memories etched in the landscapes of Lancaster, Kingston, and the United States.

Dandelion Dreams: *Tale of a Little Girl from Lancaster*

The journey continues, new adventures, challenges, and opportunities. The characters may change, and the settings may shift, but the essence of the narrative remains a testament to the transformative power of a life well-lived. As I step into the next chapter, I do so with gratitude for the past, an appreciation for the present, and an eagerness to embrace the unwritten pages of the future.

Aunty Silvie Wedding

L-R Theophilus, Saleathy, Uncle Les, Ma Lou, Aunty
Sylvie, Beverley

Auntie Sylvie at her home in Lancaster

Panseta (ME)

My wedding day on June 25, 1988

Robert Smith (Ex-husband)

My mother, Auntie Besty

Celebrating success with my beloved mother and daughter

My family, Annalise, Bobby and Belay with me

Panseta, Sheryl and Annalise

Dandelion Dreams: *Tale of a Little Girl from Lancaster*

Annalise and Belay at Disneyland Paris

Panseta Smith

Annalise graduating University of Miami, 2014, Doctor of
Philosophy in Microbiology and Immunology

Bobby graduating with BS Electrical Engineering – 2018

Panseta Smith

Bobby at NSBE Conference – 2017

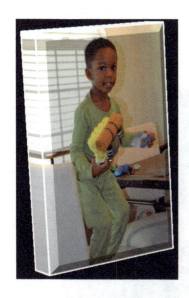

Belay- my precious grandson

Daniel and his son Kevin

Simone, Kevin's daughter.

Daniel "Danny" McIntyre – brother

Daniel and wife Rita

Kevin's son D'Andre

Kevin's son Devin

Kevin's son Damian

Daniel's son Isaac and his son Odell

Panseta Smith

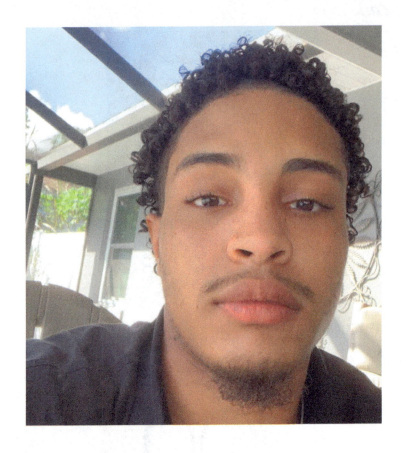

Daniel's son Moses

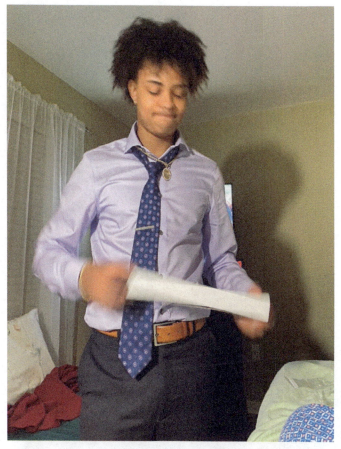

Daniel's son Jacob

Sheryl at Queens High School (Sister)

Sheryl and husband Kirk, with sons Jaden and Jaxson

Sheryl and her Husband Kirk

Sheryl, Kirk and son Jamari

Panseta Smith

Beverly Reid – Cousin

Hurley Reid, Beverly's husband

Beverly's son Rory Reid

Panseta Smith

Rural house in Jamaica. 1890s

Dandelion Dreams: *Tale of a Little Girl from Lancaster*

It described the life of a little girl growing up in Lancaster District, Manchester, Jamaica, and what it was like to be raised as a country girl. Dandelion Dreams tells the story of a grandmother's love, sacrifices, determination, and strength of character.

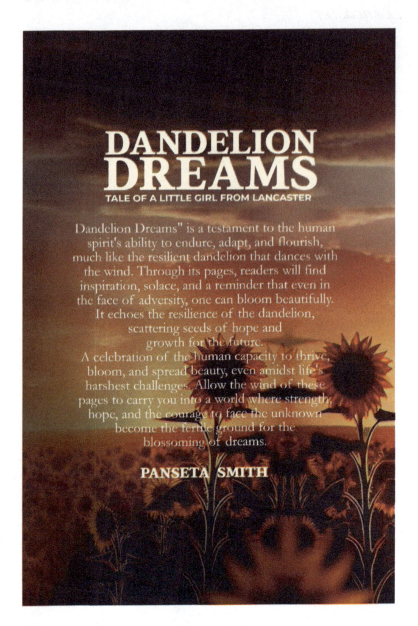

Made in the USA
Las Vegas, NV
20 March 2025

19863081R00079